# Litanies for All Occasions

# Litanies for All Occasions

### GARTH HOUSE

Judson Press®Valley Forge

LITANIES FOR ALL OCCASIONS

Copyright © 1989
Judson Press, Valley Forge, PA 19482-0851

Unless otherwise indicated, Bible quotations in this volume are from the Revised Standard Version of the Bible, copyrighted 1946, 1952, © 1971, 1973 by the Division of Christian Education of the National Council of the Churches of Christ in the U.S.A., and used by permission.

Other quotations of the Bible are from *The Holy Bible*, King James Version.

**Library of Congress Cataloging-in-Publication Data**

House, Garth.
  Litanies for all occasions / by Garth House.
      p.    cm.
  ISBN 0-8170-1144-7 : $7.50
  1. Litanies. I. Title.
BV199.L58H68   1989
264'.13—dc20                                                                89-31402
                                                                                CIP

The name JUDSON PRESS is registered as a trademark in the U.S. Patent Office.

Printed in the U.S.A.

# Litanies for All Occasions

# Dedication

For...
*Dr. Carl Brown, Dr. Marcel Hundziak, Dr. David Maze*
*and for my parents, Verl and Marylin*
*and most of all,*
*for my beloved wife, Deanna Sara Magdalena*

# Contents

# Renewal

LEADER: We who have drunk of the Lord's cup, we who have tasted of the bread of heaven, we who have felt the tender mercies of the Most High, we have no choice but to turn back again and again to our God who alone can heal our weariness.

PEOPLE: *Come, O people, let us draw near. Sons and daughters of the Most High, let us gather before our God.*

LEADER: Like newborn doves at the very first dawn, let your hearts rest in the peace of the new light that is rising in your midst.

PEOPLE: *For we are favored in God's heart, and Christ, in perfect joy, dwells in our midst.*

LEADER: Through the parched land a river flows. In the barren hills a spring breaks forth. In the empty desert a fountain rises.

PEOPLE: *On rocky ground, among the tangled thorns, along the trodden path, the seeds of the sower struggle to grow.*

LEADER: The Spirit, like a gentle rain in the summer's heat, falls quietly on God's children, nourishing the weary heart.

PEOPLE: *Sometimes it is as though our faith has no roots and withers in the world's harsh sun. Sometimes our cares and anxieties turn us away from the source of peace. Sometimes even our hope is snatched away and we are left moving blindly down a highway that seems to lead nowhere.*

LEADER: But God has not sown in vain, and God's word has not gone forward unanswered or returned without a harvest. For we are gathered here this morning, the fruit of the Spirit's activity. We have come, led by the Spirit, that we might dwell in the Spirit.

PEOPLE: *Our God points no accusing finger. Our God puts no price on the love offered to us here, although it is costly beyond all measure. Our debt is beyond our ability to*

11

*repay. God asks only that we rejoice with the hosts of heaven in the victory of love and that we accept in charity one another as God accepts us.*

LEADER: The pilgrim shout goes up and it is always new. In the kingdom the journey is always just beginning, and the saints are rising to sing as though creation had never yet echoed with the harmony of praise. The sower has never stopped casting forth seed, and whether it falls on barren rock or tangled thorns or trodden path, the Spirit in infinite tenderness nourishes its growth forever.

ALL: *We are poor in spirit, but the riches of Christ make us wealthy. We are fragile and weak, but God's Spirit gives us strength. We are sinners, but the love of Christ Jesus purifies and redeems us all. Amen.*

# Dedication of Teachers

LEADER: They called him "Rabbi," which means teacher, and he dwelt among them and taught all who came to him. He taught of things above, of the love of God for the children of humanity, of the tender compassion in God's heart for the creation, of the way we should live and grow and bear fruit for the kingdom, like seed planted in rich soil and nurtured by the gentle rains from on high.

PEOPLE: *What is a teacher, if not a mirror in which we may perceive the divine image hidden in the soul?*

LEADER: What is a teacher, if not a sower of seed and a cultivator of young gardens?

PEOPLE: *What is a teacher, if not a shaper of souls and a guide who gently shows the right path for the journey?*

LEADER: What is a teacher, if not the most hopeful of all dreamers, who plants and nurtures and sees the bright destiny and harvest of the work even when the student cannot?

PEOPLE: *What is a teacher, if not a shepherd watching over the flock and leading it to abundant pastures?*

LEADER: Dreamers and sharers of dreams, sowers of seed and guides who show the way, mirrors of goodness and shepherds of grace—it is for these teachers and this ministry, O God, that we offer our thanks.

*(silence)*

LEADER: The soul has many teachers in Christ, but who more precious than those who start us on the path, who surround the innocent heart with love and learning so that tender spirits may grow in strength and love and wisdom until they stand like cedars in a mighty forest or soar like eagles towards the heavens.

PEOPLE: *Is not life the school of the soul, and are we not all*

13

*students struggling and seeking knowledge of the Creator who is our ground, source, and destiny?*

LEADER: Are we not all signs and witnesses of the true God, mirrors of the Creator's love and words of hope spoken by the God who created heaven and earth? Are we not all teachers, one to another?

PEOPLE: *O God, bless these teachers who with such patience and hard work and commitment have glorified your name and increased the light that dwells in our midst. By your grace let us all become as those who are taught: open, alert, and attentive to the unfolding revelation of your love, that we may be learners in your kingdom.*

LEADER: From generation to generation the story of God's love is told and retold, passed down from master to disciple, from teacher to student, from parent to child, until all the families of the earth shall be full of the knowledge of God.

ALL: *All praise and honor and glory be to God who makes us a people, who gives us a story to live and to tell, who pours love and light and truth upon us until the heart sings and the soul dances. Amen.*

# Stewardship

LEADER: Who is as loyal as the God of Israel? Who so faithful as the God of our Lord, Jesus Christ?

God makes the seasons come and go. In the spring God sends the rains, and the flowers blossom. In the summer God makes the sun beam down upon the earth, and the fields flourish and ripen. In the autumn God smiles upon the harvest and watches as the people gather in the fruit of their labors. In the winter God unleashes the cold north winds to remind the children of humanity that they are mortal. Who is as loyal as the God of Israel? Who so faithful as the God of our Lord, Jesus Christ?

PEOPLE: *Our hearts are steadfast, O Lord, our hearts are steadfast. We gather here this morning because you have called us. In your mercy and by your grace accept us as we are: ignorant, frail, imperfect, even confused. We are certain of one thing only—we need you. We need your love, your guidance, your mercy, and your faithfulness.*

LEADER: All people are grass; they last no longer than a flower of the field. The grass withers, the flowers fade when the breath of the Lord blows upon them; the grass withers, the flowers fade, but the word of our God endures forevermore.[1]

PEOPLE: *Without you, Lord, we are nothing. Who are we to declare our loyalty? Who are we to make vows of faithfulness? Who are we to promise our love? Who are we to dare to hope? Yet because you, Lord, are loyal, we can be loyal. Because you are faithful, we can be faithful. Because you give us hope, we can hope. Because you loved us first, we can love you and one another. For our hope, our love, and our loyalty are gifts from you.*

15

ALL: *So strengthen us, Lord, for the tasks ahead; bind us closely to your side; take us by the hand and lead us through this world. At this time of commitment and rededication, let our vows of loyalty to this church, to your kingdom, to one another, and to all humanity be not empty words, but*

*rather harbingers of lives lived in loyalty and obedience*
*to you. In your name, Jesus, do we pray, amen.*

[1]Isaiah 40:6-8, paraphrased

# Thanksgiving

LEADER: Through these doors have stumbled pilgrims, outcasts, unwashed saints, sin-wounded sisters and brothers, the rich and the impoverished, people with the learning of ages, and children with only the word of love at their command; a thousand Magdalenes and a thousand Simon Peters have stumbled through these doors, all crying out for shelter from a raging storm, each seeking a balm for wounds they could not even name.

FIRST READER: Raise high the roof beam of God's house!

SECOND READER: For mercy dwells where the flame of grace is kindled and is kept.

THIRD READER: And love doth make its nest among a people of steadfast compassion.

PEOPLE: *We are a colony of heaven, a redeemed people, a royal priesthood, a ministering body of God's healing grace, a sacred isle of peace, and a beacon of hope in a broken and suffering world.*

LEADER: Who would sing the humility and unassuming love of God's servants? Who can number the countless deeds of kindness and gentle caring that minister to each passing day of this dawning sovereignty of new heavens and new earth? Who would count the threads of this invisible tapestry of prayer with which we are knit together and under which we rest, tabernacled in love?

FIRST READER: Sing, angels of grace, and break forth you ministers of mercy. For God has chosen and formed a people.

**17**

SECOND READER: The Spirit has been bestowed and shall not be taken back.

THIRD READER: What God has given you no power in heaven or earth can take away.

PEOPLE: *What love is this? What grace, what joyful bliss that we are found awake and at our watch. What joy that our names are penned forever in the book of God's eternal life.*

LEADER: We shall not die, but live to tell the story of God's unconquerable love, to sing and dance to the graceful rhythms of kingdom lutes and tambours—that all generations of God's children shall see and know the salvation of our God, in whose hands the swelling oceans and rolling plains, the towering cities and quiet village streets, the forests and the fields rest under the dawning light of a new heaven.

FIRST READER: Hosanna in the highest to the victory of our God.

SECOND READER: God's justice and God's peace fall upon the children of humanity as summer rain in gentleness ends a cruel drought.

THIRD READER: Hosanna in the highest to the victory of our God.

ALL: *Heavens may pass away. Offerings of grain and of our bounty may cease. Kings and royal families may rise and fall, tides sweep in and sweep out, forests grow and pass away, suns die and new suns be born.*

LEADER: But Christ's church shall never be defeated. Like the phoenix from a holy tree, the church shall rise again and again and again, until the word of God's love runs deep in every heart of all that lives and breathes.

ALL: *And all creation will be holy and the hosannas of our thanksgiving shall rise unto the heavens for ever and ever. Amen.*

Dedicated to the University Baptist Church of Columbus, Ohio, on the occasion of their twentieth year of ministry on West Lane Avenue.

# First Sunday of Advent

LEADER: The bounty of summer has been harvested. The birds have fled south. The leaves have fallen from the trees. The cold winds blow, and all nature stands shorn of her riches.

PEOPLE: *O Lord, in this season of expectation and waiting, strip from our hearts all anxiety and worldly distractions so that we may be pure and open vessels to receive the precious gifts you have promised to us. As nature dies only to be reborn in spring, let us become poor in ourselves in order that we may become rich in the wealth only you can give.*

LEADER: As certain as the coming dawn, as reliable as the stars in their courses, so are the promises of God given to God's sons and daughters. And what has God promised to the servants that are gathered here this morning?

PEOPLE: *To us, God's servants, God has promised a leader, one who would guide us and counsel us, one who would share our joys and our sorrows, one who would never abandon us, one whose sojourn on earth would serve as a sign that hope and love will never be vanquished. By our very presence here this day we bear witness that this promise of God has been fulfilled. Jesus of Nazareth is our Lord and Savior, and in him do we hope and trust.*

LEADER: And what has God promised to the children of humankind, even to all humanity?

PEOPLE: *That the poor and the outcast shall be raised up and incorporated into community. That the powerless and voiceless shall be heard in the councils of the mighty. That the instruments of war and destruction shall be transformed into the tools of peace. That disease and suffering shall come to an end. That peace and reconciliation shall dawn upon all peoples in this tormented world. That the wolf shall feed with the lamb, and the lion eat straw like the ox,[1] and the*

19

[1]Isaiah 65:25, paraphrased

*whole earth be full of the knowledge of the Lord, even as the
waters cover the sea.*[2]

LEADER: So we wait, O God, for the fullness of time when all this shall
come to pass. Yet even as we wait, we are already blessed. In
being blessed let not our waiting be mere idleness.

PEOPLE: *As we wait upon your gifts, O God, gifts that are ever new,
let us use the gifts you have already bestowed upon us. Let
us serve and heal, minister and console, liberate and raise
up. During this Advent season, empower us to be your
co-workers in bringing to reality the promises you have
made to all humanity. In Jesus' name we pray, amen.*

[2]Isaiah 11:9, paraphrased

20

# Second Sunday of Advent

LEADER: "Be still, and know that I am God," says the Lord.[1]

*(silence)*

FIRST READER: The owl sits in the moonlight and knows the quiver of every blade of grass and the silent roaring conflagration of every distant star.

SECOND READER: The little boy hears the steady drumming of the summer rain, pulls the downy covers over his head, and knows that he is safe.

THIRD READER: And the businesswoman with so much on her mind suddenly looks up to see the geese sailing like a dream of freedom over the office building in the morning.

LEADER: O be still and quiet, people of God, and the Spirit, like a trembling deer, will venture into the clearing of your heart.

PEOPLE: *We have rushed about the temple of the world like priests preparing for a siege, like mad generals destroying documents before a retreat, like dazzled children on the morning of gifts rushing from one half-opened present to another.*

LEADER: It is not so with those who wait upon God. For only in the silent turning of her heart did Mary hear the angel speak, and only under the speechless silence of the stars did shepherds hear the gathered hosts break forth in song.

FIRST READER: And only in the emptiness outside the gates can one hear God's heart break amid hurled contempt and the echoed blows of hammer and spike.

21

LEADER: Blessed are the people who wait upon God, who feast in silent gladness upon the bread of their salvation and share the goodness of their blessing with fellow beggars who, like themselves, know the infinite wealth of God's mercy in the poverty of their own emptiness.

PEOPLE: *You have called, O God, and we have come. You have blessed, and we have responded. You have judged. We have repented. Before us at our feet you have cast your heart.*

FIRST READER: What love is this?

SECOND READER: What mercy?

THIRD READER: What gentle bliss?

PEOPLE: *That our Christ should with us await the kingdom dawn and with us warm his hands around our common fire.*

LEADER: Like the whistle of a slow-moving freight at dawn that wakes us from a night of rest unto a choir of morning sparrows, so the kingdom's call will go forth across the land.

FIRST READER: Does it not already echo across the valleys of our blessedness?

SECOND READER: Do not its still and dulcet notes yet hang suspended in the beams of morning light?

THIRD READER: Have not the sparrow and the hawk, the bear and running elk heard the matin call?

LEADER: The advent of our deliverance is at hand. Our salvation is upon us. Lift up your hearts! Raise your countenance to this world on which the wealth of God has been spent.

ALL: *All glory, laud and honor be to God, who like a mother gathering her children calls us together in grace, or like the soaring eagle keeps watch over her brood and with talons sharp and fierce fends off those who would do us harm. Her love and tender mercies cannot be defeated as we await the unfolding sovereignty of new heavens and new earth. Amen.*

22

[1]Psalm 46:10

# Third Sunday of Advent

LEADER: This is the season of giving and receiving. This is the time of waiting and hoping. These are days full of joyous expectation. Yet who is more eager to give than the Lord? Who more patient than God? Who more full of joy than Jesus Christ?

PEOPLE: *O Lord, as we prepare to celebrate your birthday, purify us, consecrate us, and humble us that our hearts may be open to receive the immeasurable happiness you long so passionately to give us. In this world of broken dreams and crushed hopes, grant us, O Lord, the courage to dream the great dream of your kingdom. Grant us the strength that, with your help, will enable us to bring that dream to reality. And in your mercy, O Lord, grant us the privilege of awakening humanity from the nightmare of despair and hopelessness to the glorious dream of hope and love promised by the prophets and by you.*

LEADER: The world says "Fools! Those who dare to love end up being hurt. Those who dare to hope end up being disappointed. Those who dare to dream end up being deluded. We shall horde our love, resign our hopes, ignore our dreams. We shall become wise and prudent. We shall risk nothing."

PEOPLE: *But the word of the Lord says:*

> *Then the eyes of the blind shall be opened,*
>   *and the ears of the deaf unstopped;*
> *then shall the lame man leap like a hart,*
>   *and the tongue of the dumb sing for joy.*
> *For waters shall break forth in the wilderness,*
>   *and streams in the desert;*
> *the burning sand shall become a pool,*
>   *and the thirsty ground springs of water....*
> *And the ransomed of the* LORD *shall return,*
>   *and come to Zion with singing;*
> *everlasting joy shall be upon their heads;*

*they shall obtain joy and gladness,*
*and sorrow and sighing shall flee away.*[1]

**ALL:** *Amen.*

[1]Isaiah 35:5-7, 10

# Fourth Sunday of Advent

ALL: *Lord, we are grateful for every evidence of your love.*

LEADER: In spring we are surrounded on all sides with the beauty and energy of a garden bursting with the vitality of life. In summer we find nature sunk in a deep dreaming slumber, exhausted by her own creativity. In autumn nature is filled with the dazzling melancholy and longing of the harvesttime when each tree explodes in an encore of color, and, in one final gesture, she casts her glorious raiments on the earth.

PEOPLE: *For God so loved the world...*

LEADER: But in winter nature withholds her evidence, and we must look to the human countenance of our family and friends to find the reassurance of love against the indifference in the world. In the candle of human love, glowing in the wintry night as the winds moan and howl outside, we find our humanity, and in so doing, we experience God's intimate love, a love that understands its own frail vulnerability and its own infinite source.

PEOPLE: *For God so loved the world that on a wintry night long ago, a child was born in the poverty, darkness, and cold of a stable.*

LEADER: He felt the cold of a winter night, experienced the mystery of a star-filled heaven, and knew the weariness and pain and sorrow of a broken world.

PEOPLE: *Dearest Lord, lift up our hearts that we might behold the mystery of your love, a love that will not let us go, a love so passionate that we are captives to it all of our lives, a love that fathoms and comprehends the highest pinnacle of our joy and the darkest valley of our grief.*

25

LEADER: "As the rain and the snow come down from heaven,
    and return not thither but water the earth,
  making it bring forth and sprout,

giving seed to the sower and bread to the
    eater,
so shall my word be that goes forth from my
    mouth;
it shall not return to me empty,
but it shall accomplish that which I purpose,
    and prosper in the thing for which I sent it."[1]

PEOPLE: *Amen.*

[1]Isaiah 55:10-11

# Christmas Eve—Communion

LEADER: Like pilgrim shepherds we have gathered tonight. Like children of royalty we have come together to celebrate the birth of true royalty.

PEOPLE: *Our Savior comes to us as a babe, wrapped in swaddling cloths. He lays aside his crown to dwell among us and share the joy and sorrow of our pilgrimage. He passes through the curtain around God's love and, holding it aside, invites us in.*

LEADER: Oh, the humanity of God, the divinity of God's children.

PEOPLE: *What child is this? What love is this that seeks to share our burdens and lead us on in kindness towards a glory that is gentle and peaceful like a meadow in spring?*

LEADER: O God, roll away the stone in our hearts and let our spirits soar into that realm where angels laugh, martyrs weep for joy, and God's infinite love dances among the singing throngs of those who have gone before us.

PEOPLE: *That we may know what has been accomplished in this child, that we may see the world as you see it, Lord, sanctified, cleansed, and sojourning towards a healing so great we are almost afraid to hope in it.*

LEADER: On the night before his death, Jesus said to his disciples, "I have earnestly desired to eat this passover with you before I suffer."[1] Now the risen Christ, in perfect joy, graciously invites us to join him at the table, to break and share the bread of life and lift with him the cup of salvation.

PEOPLE: *O Lord, as we join you at your table on this sacred eve, accept us as we are, even in all of our imperfections.*

LEADER: Jesus says: "Come unto me, all ye that labour and are heavy laden, and I will give you rest. Take my yoke upon you, and learn of me; for I am meek and lowly in heart: and ye shall find rest

27

unto your souls."[2]

PEOPLE: *What shall we render to the Lord for all God's bounty to us?*
*We shall lift the cup of salvation and call on the name of the*
*Lord.*

ALL: *This Christmastide let our spirits so entwine that we form*
*a wreath of joy, a circle of light from which God's precious*
*and fragile love will shine out into the darkness of this*
*world and into our own hearts. It is in the strong name of*
*Jesus, who came to us as a child, that we ask this. Amen.*

[1]Luke 22:14
[2]Matthew 11:28-29 (KJV)

# The New Year

LEADER: Proclaim not just the turning of the calendar or the circling motion of the stars. Proclaim not just some senseless celebration of time passing or some wild conflagration of our pasts. Proclaim instead the beginning of our jubilation and the passing away of fear. Proclaim the radiance of salvation fulfilled, which even now rolls in waves around this world with the swiftness of sunlight racing across the verdant fields of a righteous generation.

PEOPLE: *The frame of this world is passing away. Rivers of healing are breaking forth where once were only broken glass and concrete. Fountains of hope are springing up in dry places. In desert places the waters of hope flow forth.*

LEADER: I say to you: Proclaim not just a new year, but proclaim new heavens and new earth. Testify to new hearts liberated from the chains of shame and fear. Lift up your hearts and begin again, purified of the past like a meadow dripping with spring rain.

PEOPLE: *This is the work of our God: that we can arrive over and over at the beginning, our past behind us and forgiven—a storehouse of memory and beauty and instruction, not a manacle of shame to keep us from the future.*

LEADER: That future is here. The kingdom has begun and is upon us. The new year stretches out before us like a long, slow journey through mountain nights of dancing fiestas and days where time drips slowly like honey.

Eternity has begun. Smash the bonds of broken sorrows and disappointments of your past and give yourself to the kingdom road stretched out before you.

29

PEOPLE: *Hosanna in the highest to our God who leads us forward on the pilgrim march. Surely with the light dwelling in our midst we shall reach our home, and the spark that lit the flames shall not be lost along the way.*

LEADER: Blow the trumpet of our jubilee! Let this new year see the walls of greed and selfishness fall forever before the onrushing waters of God's justice.

PEOPLE: *Let the new year trumpet forth a kingdom come in ever-dawning glory, and raise a song of freedom for all the peoples of the world.*

LEADER: Let us drink fully and completely of the cup of each unfolding day of this new year, drink deeply of the beauty and the joy of life's unutterable mystery.

PEOPLE: *Let us drink deeply of life's dreaming beauty until we are so intoxicated with God's love and creation's awesome majesty that whether we are dreaming or awake, reality shall from poetry and beauty be inseparable, and creation will have returned to what it was before.*

ALL: *Each year our kingdom hope is born anew. Go forth, therefore, to do God's holy work, and the harvest of this coming year will outstrip the wildest hopes of our imagining. Amen.*

# Martin Luther King, Jr., Day

LEADER: Under the hot Atlanta sun, in the midst of blue waters, the white sepulchre rests. The words carved in marble do not ring or echo off the glass towers of the cities or roll across the quilted plains of our overflowing blessedness.

The shadowed fist of hatred and violence has shattered and stilled the music of his voice, and now his words in silence, mute as stone, await the kindling flame of those who, like himself, can banish fear into its narrow cell and loose the soul for love's unconquerable power.

PEOPLE: *Who dares to lift the song of justice in unjust and dangerous times...*

LEADER: ...when unspoken and unadmitted fear sends us bowing down to the shadow power of shadow gods which the hidden courage of the heart holds in contempt?

PEOPLE: *Who dares to lift up the song of justice in these times?*

LEADER: Once the bells of freedom have rung, once one person has stood fearless before the smooth and sightless engine of oppression...

PEOPLE: *...and felt the crosshairs of the rifle sighted on his brow,...*

LEADER: ...once one person has stood without fear before injustice and felt the focused aim of death, and yet gone on, once the bells of freedom have rung out and broken forth upon the land, once justice has begun to roll down like waters—only then can love become sovereign and rule gently from sea to shining sea in this sweet land of liberty. Your daughters and your sons stand before their God and fear flees away. Mighty love of Christ, descend into their souls as a flock of doves might glide onto the shining meadows of the dawn.

31

Brothers and sisters, children of God, we have been to the mountain heights; we have seen the promised land.

PEOPLE: *Amen.*

LEADER: Indeed, the afterglow of dawn yet paints the rising peaks behind us with roses and with pearls. Let us descend the downward slopes into the valleys of the kingdom.

PEOPLE: *Amen.*

LEADER: Cradle your brother, lift up your sister, bind up the wounded.

PEOPLE: *Amen.*

LEADER: Lift up the pipes of peace and shoulder, each one, the cross beams of our victory. For we shall build anew the cities of our God and reap the harvest of God's joy among the valleys of grace.

PEOPLE: *Amen.*

LEADER: Each one shall help the other, and we shall be keepers of each and every precious child of God. The blood that flows among us will not touch the soil, but rather, like a singing river that draws a silver circle around a sacred isle, it will bind us to one another in one sacred unity of gentleness and love.

PEOPLE: *Amen.*

LEADER: The dawn has come at last. The pealing of the freedom bells cascades from the hills and rolls like mighty rivers into the desert of the past. In our midst the light has dwelt and journeyed with us through the grief and sorrow, the joy and love of our pilgrimage.

PEOPLE: *Amen.*

LEADER: Let that light now shine from every face of every child, from every brother and every sister, every father, every mother—that every continent of this verdant earth shall be strewn with the glowing fires of freedom and liberty. And the glory of the heavens will be envious of the jeweled earth, which will chart its course among the fiery novas of the unvierse.

ALL: *Amen and amen.*

# Ash Wednesday

LEADER: Let us return to the Lord and his ways, brothers and sisters.

PEOPLE: *Yes, let us return unto the Lord. Let us bring joy to God's countenance that God may slay the fatted calf and rejoice in our return.*

LEADER: Let us not waste our time in preparing a defense or in hating ourselves or in pondering the wounds of our guilt and despair.

PEOPLE: *Let us cast it all at his feet—he whose love aches for us, he who hovers over us in longing, he who waits for our turning that he may seize us in his arms and take to his own heart the pain and brokenness of our lives.*

LEADER: O Lord, we have traveled far together. The faith of our youth has grown dull. Our eye has grown dim, and the beauty and mystery of your creation do not speak to us as they once did.

PEOPLE: *O Lord, the fire of our love for you has grown weak. Our hearts have become hardened. Our love is narrow and confined. We have become stingy with our affections, and in the darkness of this world we seek your light less and less often.*

LEADER: Lord have mercy.

PEOPLE: *Christ have mercy.*

LEADER: Lord have mercy. Are we not like grasshoppers trying to understand the sun?

PEOPLE: *Is not life like a flask of rich wine too quickly consumed? Are we not like the flower of the field, blossoming for a moment, then swept away?*

LEADER: The God of our Lord Jesus says to us that it is not so: "I give Egypt as your ransom, Ethiopia and Seba in exchange for you. Because you are precious in my eyes, and honored, and I love you,[1] I will give you to my only son, he who is closest to my heart, that you

33

might know and believe how deep is my love for you."

PEOPLE: *We are but dust, O Lord.*

LEADER: But we have been chosen for an immortal destiny.

PEOPLE: *We are but flesh, O Lord.*

LEADER: But God's Spirit rests upon us.

PEOPLE: *We are but sinners, O Lord.*

ALL: *But the grace of Jesus Christ sanctifies all of us. Amen.*

[1]Isaiah 43:3,4

# Lent

LEADER: Beneath the ice of frozen rivers, waters run—onrushing, turbulent, and silent. Beneath the shroud of snow, tubers stir, seeds burst, unseen and unheard. Above the dull blanket of clouds light pours forth, but only the soaring eagle feels its warmth or sees its splendor.

PEOPLE: *For three dark, futureless days they huddled together behind locked doors. Having abandoned him, they were trapped in the city, themselves abandoned, full of fear, shame, grief, self-hatred, and despair.*

LEADER: How gently spring blows her clarion over the dreaming earth! First it is only the cheerful songs of birds, which we seem not to have heard for months. Then the slow, steady dripping of melting snow on the ledge outside the window. Then the hiss of tires on wet asphalt and the quiet murmur of water in the gutters. How gently spring blows her bright clarion over the dreaming earth!

PEOPLE: *This winter has been long and hard, O Lord. The cold, gray days have followed one another with dreary monotony as though the warmth and abundant life of nature were some vague and distant dream we would never taste again. Such are the days when we cannot feel your love, O God, when there seems to be no future for us, when our hearts seem as cold as the frozen river and our voices of praise as silent as the barren trees.*

LEADER: That evening Christ came to them, breathing peace into their hearts and gently mocking their lack of faith. In the stillness and radiance of that presence, in that roar of silence and light, the ice cracked and the waters of mercy and love flowed—infinite, abundant, unstoppable—into the sea of history.

35

PEOPLE: *Abide with us, O Lord, and sojourn with us as we journey with you toward Jerusalem. We shall make our ascent with you to the Holy City, and this time we shall be with you and you with us when together we climb that hill to plant our cross, knowing that on the other side lies the eternal ocean, and on its shore stands Miriam,[1] timbrel raised above her head.*

[1]Miriam—the sister of Moses, who danced and sang on the shore of the Red Sea after the children of Israel were delivered from Pharaoh's horsemen.

# Lenten Vespers

LEADER: We have each gone our own way. You have, and you have, and I have, too. We have each run laughing through that tall grass that sang with the August crickets and swayed in drunken ecstasy beneath the sweet breath of summer—while the exhausted father set up the tent, built the fire, cooked the evening meal, and gently and carefully prepared our beds.

PEOPLE: *We have each gone our own way. Christ have mercy. We have each gone our own way.*

LEADER: We have each, at least once, failed utterly the sister or brother whom we loved beyond words, who believed in us beyond doubt and fear, and who never stopped loving us.

PEOPLE: *Lord have mercy. We have each gone our own way.*

LEADER: We have each chosen, at least once, the path of disobedience. We have each, at least once, sat angry and dissatisfied in the midst of costly and precious gifts that our mother spent an excited night wrapping...Love cannot be defeated, my friends.

PEOPLE: *Christ have mercy. We have all gone our own way.*

LEADER: We stand outside the door behind which father and mother, brothers and sisters wait in breathless joy around the flaming candles on the cake that bears each of our names, names they cherish.

PEOPLE: *Did he not say, "Ask, and it will be given you;...knock, and it will be opened to you"?*[1]

LEADER: From the mountains and from the valley floors, from the sweeping plains and rolling hills we have been called; we have been called together from out of our own way into the way of love.

Every silent reach of sorrow, every secret wound of shame, every

---

[1]Matthew 7:7

fear, and every laughing joy that rests within the hidden chambers of our hearts is known unto Christ who stands among us now in perfect joy and commands that we cast off our fear and shame and enter in the kingdom door to find that family to which we belong if we but knock and enter in.

PEOPLE: *A being of sorrow and of grief, God's child has felt and tasted the death and pain, the love and joy that knit together our human frame.*

ALL: *What love is this, O God, what love is this that like a brother's faith, a sister's tears, a father's kindness, or a mother's strength bears the heavy freight of our own broken love so that we, a purchased people, might enter in the door of grace and dwell within the realm of light that shines from Love's redeeming face. Amen.*

# Palm Sunday

FIRST READER: Let laughter turn to tears and choirs of angels hold their peace. Let trumpets drop and tambours cease.

SECOND READER: Let women clasp their babes tightly to their breasts and men and boys scurry to the shelter of closed doors and guarded windows.

THIRD READER: Let the breeze fall to stillness and singing birds keep their silence. Let all that is grand and noble and full of great drama fall away and vanish.

LEADER: And let the city be a city without title, rank, or fame. Let the road be any road, a dusty path without a name. Let no history guild the walls and parapets with glory or special honor, and in the awful silence of his passion entry let all sound and shouted cries fall away until one can hear a truthful word of love whispered between you and me.

FIRST READER: For it is not of star-strewn heavens that we sing nor snow-capped peaks of far-flung mountain ranges nor mighty herds of elk that roam the plains nor myriad flocks of doves that sail the coastal seas.

SECOND READER: Nor does our song ring with the majesty of mighty deeds of conquest or fierce battles fought and won.

THIRD READER: No. It's scope is only human in its range.

PEOPLE: *For God's child, like us, knew the night so endlessly cold and the hope and warmth that came with dawn. This child knew shame and love's healing power, the soaring joy of children joined in song and the broken sorrow of his own* 39 *and others' broken love.*

FIRST READER: Like a hunted child he knew the fear that runs like a river of ice in a bottomless gorge, and he also knew the fearless courage of having crossed over the fragile bridge suspended out in darkness.

LEADER: But who can tell the pain and anger of such a heart held out to a blind and selfish generation, a generation of judges and not of lovers, a generation of guarded stinginess and not of his own limitless generosity.

PEOPLE: *And so he rode into the city, one last gift brought to the altar of a blind generation, one last offering of his heart before a selfish, fear-torn people caught up in the worship of hollow, empty gods.*

LEADER: How many times has the king of glory ridden defenseless and vulnerable among a people of cold and hardened hearts, a faithless people caught up in the scramble to secure and keep for themselves a wealth and security built on shifting sands, as transient as the grass of the field?

PEOPLE: *Every time we turn away from a brother or sister in need or bring down judgment where love should reign or shun exuberant generosity in exchange for worldly calculation or loan out our love tangled with strings of conditions and demands—each time we do this our Christ again turns toward Jerusalem and begins the ascent of deep sorrow.*

FIRST READER: How long must he endure our lukewarm faith and our tepid passion?

SECOND READER: How long can love be measured out in teaspoons?

THIRD READER: How long before love pours forth upon us all like a rain of healing fire?

LEADER: People of .God, your Christ will not enter your city, will not enter your house, will not find entry into the holy place of your heart until every time that your life crosses another, until the hello of all your days is accompanied by your silent hosanna:

**40**

ALL: *In the name of the Lord this person comes to me. Blessed is this person who comes to me in the name of the Lord. Amen.*

# Tenebrae/Maundy Thursday

FIRST READER: Watchman, what of the night?

SECOND READER: It is dark and cold, and the Son of God has been handed over to men who call themselves righteous.

FIRST READER: Then his reign is assured, is it not?

PEOPLE: *No, no. They spat upon him and beat him with their fists and handed him over to be crucified.*

FIRST READER: But where were his followers and his friends?

SECOND READER: They abandoned him and denied him.

PEOPLE: *Lord, in our moment of darkness and at the hour of our death forgive us our cowardice, our weakness, and our lack of faith.*

FIRST READER: Watchman, what of the night?

SECOND READER: Dawn approaches, but promises no light.

PEOPLE: *Sweet Jesus, Lord of light, let our tears wash your wounds and dissolve all your memories of pain, despair, and abandonment.*

ALL: *Amen.*

# Good Friday

**LEADER:** O darkness, darkness!
The Son of God is crucified.
Who was there with him at the cross?

**WOMEN:** *We were there with him at the cross. We followed him from Galilee. We served him and waited upon him. We washed his feet with our tears and anointed his head with oil. We saw them drive the nails. We heard him cry out. We were there with him at the cross.*

**MEN:** *We were there with him at the cross. Soldiers and leaders, we drove the nails; we drew the lots for his clothing; we hurled abuse at him. We were there with him at the cross.*

**LEADER:** How long, O Lord, how long must it be thus with men the executioners and women the weeping witnesses? Transport me to a place where this is no longer true. Where men are reconciled to women: husband to wife, lover to beloved, brother to sister.

**ALL:** *We are a colony of heaven. We were there at the cross, and we have learned the lesson of the cross. We are reconciled one to another: husband to wife, lover to beloved, brother to sister.*

*We are a colony of heaven, and we have learned the lesson of the cross. Amen.*

# Easter

LEADER: The nightmare is over. The hour of darkness has passed. God's mercy and love have triumphed once and for all over humankind's hatred and ignorance. Miracle of miracles, you have come back to us, O Lord, to us who failed you so utterly at the cross. And you have brought with you not judgment, but the peace of eternal life.

PEOPLE: *The risen Christ is with us. Guide us, O Lord, into the ways of truth. Empower us, O Lord, with the gifts of the Holy Spirit. Teach us, O Lord, how we may serve one another and serve your church…*

LEADER: …Your church, O Lord, which through the ages you have inspired and led. As we gather together to do the work of the church, to sustain not only its spiritual health but its material existence, continue to be with us and guide us so that we may be worthy of your love and your church may continue to be a fountain of light and healing in a dark and broken world.

PEOPLE: *We are the chosen servants of the Lord. We are the mystical body of Christ. We have been granted the privilege and responsibility to carry on the redemptive work of Jesus. Let us go forward in love and humility to serve and strengthen the church. Amen.*

# The Sunday After Easter

LEADER: The gnarled olivewood, stained dark by the weeping heavens, drinks in the gentle sunlight of a spring morning. A cock crows in the distance; sparrows gather grass and flit about their nests; flowers tremble in the soft breeze; and by the empty tomb the kneeling soldier will not rise.

On the hill the crosses stand, empty now, drying in the sun, robbed of their shame by a love wounded and broken and risen in a glory as peaceful as the dove in flight.

PEOPLE: *Since that day, from generation to generation the Lord has walked with his servants and has called men and women of all races, of all ages, from every culture and every condition of life, into the mystery of his love.*

LEADER: In a century in which death has reigned, whole peoples have perished, famine rages, and the nations offer the fruit of the harvest on the altar of weaponry and armament, a century in which justice has disintegrated into the indiscriminate madness of terrorism by individuals and nations, where is the kingdom to be found and where is a person to find the community of compassion in an indifferent and uncaring world?

PEOPLE: *We are known not by our numbers and not by our wealth nor by our power and knowledge. Only by the love and compassion and caring we bring to each other and to all God's as yet ungathered children are we faithful to our Lord. Only by that love do we offer to the anguished people of the world a hope and a dream that even death cannot shatter.*

LEADER: With what sweet gentleness the swallow lifts her wings in the spring evening. In the falling twilight laughing children are called home and reluctantly tear themselves away from breathless shadows. In a car stopped at an intersection, windows down and radio playing, a young man and woman kiss, oblivious to all else. The ducks have landed in the river; the winter's crop of one- and two-year olds totter along before strolling parents, and the trees reach leafless and heavy with buds toward the pale moon set in the azure sky.

PEOPLE: *The glory of creation is the evidence of God's love.*

LEADER: Like the rhythm of the ocean, God's people gather together, then scatter, then gather together again. Like a sigh of infinite joy, the Spirit moves among God's servants, touching one to laughter, another to deep prayer. Creation and the world go on their way toward that secret destiny so hard to believe in and hope for, and the people of God laugh and weep and dance their way in and towards the kingdom.

ALL: *Amen.*

48

# Pentecost

LEADER: O wind that sways no branches, fire that does not burn, unimaginable light that does not blind, fountain of life that has no end, infinite river of joy, flawless mirror of God's power, kind laughing agent of God's mirth, gentle consolation of God's mercy, O Holy Spirit of God, abide with your people; come to us now in the peace of your son, Jesus.

*(silence)*

The dove glides through the morning air and flutters gently onto the nest built by God's children.

PEOPLE: *Lord, once we were poor, now we are wealthy; once we were isolated wanderers, now we are a royal people; once lost in confusion, now we are gathered in clarity and love.*

LEADER: The Holy Spirit chose not the corridors of power and wealth, neither the hallways of palaces or mansions. The Savior sought out neither the kings and princes nor the successful and righteous of this world. Christ came from the immeasurable height of God's majesty to walk sandle-shod in the dusty roads seeking the poor, the outcast, the sick; to make whole what was broken; to heal what was sick; and to bring light where there was darkness, give hope where there was despair, and redeem what had been lost.

PEOPLE: *O Lord, we are here this morning drawn by the mysterious operation of your Spirit. We remember that your church was born in wind and fire, not to sweep us heavenward like a presumptuous tower, but to guide us down the dusty roads of this world so that we may lift up the downcast, heal the broken, reconcile what is lost, and bring peace amidst unrest.*

49

LEADER: The Spirit of God broods over creation and longs to enter the hearts of God's servants. The light seeks out the darkness and longs to be kindled anew in the vessels of its choosing. Too many lamps are hidden under meal tubs, and too many flames flicker and grow weak.

PEOPLE: *Let us be born again, O Lord. Let the fire of your love and the wind of your Spirit sweep through us again.*

LEADER: Let your church be renewed and your servants revived.

PEOPLE: *Open our eyes and our ears and our hearts that we may perceive the ceaseless activity of your Spirit in us and around us.*

LEADER: Let love and reconciliation flow among us like new wine.

PEOPLE: *Let the flame of compassion consume bitterness and strife, that the unity of love will prevail.*

LEADER: And Lord, if you would give us tongues to speak, then let our common language be that of kindness and love, of mutual honor and forgiveness. For we seek not to build a tower, but rather to mend and heal a world, to unify a people.

*(silence)*

Spirit of beauty, Spirit of love, Spirit of hope, comforting Spirit, healing Spirit, patient Spirit, Spirit of peace, Holy Spirit of God, descend upon our hearts and abide now and forevermore.

ALL: *Amen.*

# Memorial Day

LEADER: Once in our firstborn innocence we ran shouting onto the fields of praise, and, breathless, we plunged into life as though sorrow and brokenness would never find us out.

PEOPLE: *How fragile we are, O God, and yet how strong you make us through the cross of your Son.*

LEADER: Spring came early at Cana in Galilee, and at the wedding feast the wine glowed ruby red in the sunlight. It was as though a river of joy had suddenly sprung forth from parched earth.

PEOPLE: *How fragile we are, O God, and yet how strong you make us through the cross of your Son.*

LEADER: Now we know what it is like to sit by the waters of Babylon, to wander through the barren wilderness, to stumble and fall beneath a cross beam of sorrow and grief so heavy that we cannot bear it alone.

PEOPLE: *How vulnerable we are, O God, and yet how strong you make us through the cross of your Son.*

LEADER: The springtime of Galilee seemed far away as they made their ascent toward Jerusalem, in the dust and the harsh sunlight. At Bethany he wept in grief; in the garden he prayed in anguish. In the morning between the praetorium and Golgotha, he stumbled and fell, unable to bear his own cross.

PEOPLE: *The word became flesh and dwelt among us. Our grief is God's grief. Our sorrow is God's sorrow. And God's strength is our strength.*

51

LEADER: The baptism of life is a baptism of beauty and sorrow, of love and grief, of receiving and letting go. And where there is baptism, there is new life.

PEOPLE: *Where there is new life, there is resurrection.*

LEADER: Where there is resurrection, there is the power of God.

PEOPLE: *Where there is the power of God, there is healing.*

LEADER: Where there is healing, there is love.

PEOPLE: *Where there is love, there is strength.*

LEADER: O God, we your people are but sojourners in this world. How far away from home we feel at this moment. Abide with us in the pain of our loss. Draw close to us in the emptiness of our grief.

PEOPLE: *We stand in need of you, O God. How fragile we are, O Lord, yet what strength you give us through your cross.*

LEADER: In the high mountains the snow is melting, and in the cathedral of towering rocks the cascading waters echo like a choir of laughing children. The waters tumble into the river, and the river flows from the valley onto the plain. The skies are filled with flocks of birds returning home, and in the dawn outside our windows they call us toward a new morning. The heavens water the wounded earth, and soon her scars are healed by a mantle of green. The gentle breath of spring whispers a promise to the budding trees, and the stars pour down their light in silence.

In the green depth of the forest a tiny day lily opens its petals and drinks in the light of a single sunbeam. Above, in the shaft of light, dances a blue butterfly. And the people of God arise and go forth, for the One who is the way and the truth and the resurrection and the life calls unto them saying, "Come, let us go forward."

In memory of Morgan McCullough.

# Independence Day

LEADER: The forests and the streams, the rivers and the meadows, the valleys and the mountains, the fields brimming with wheat and corn, the great cities with their towering skyscrapers of steel and glass, the small towns with their rising steeples witnessing to your presence among us—truly, O God, ours is a land that you have blessed abundantly.

PEOPLE: *Accept our prayer of thanksgiving, O God, for the marvelous land you have given us to dwell in.*

*(silence)*

LEADER: Many years ago the founders of our country gathered in Philadelphia to initiate a new experiment in government. They were people of faith—faith in the providence of God and the competence of all citizens to manage their own destiny—and possessed a vision of a land where the human spirit, created free and owing ultimate allegiance only to the Creator, would be free to reach its highest potential.

PEOPLE: *We are heirs of that faith and that vision. Yet we know that unless the Lord keeps watch over a nation, in vain the watchman stands on guard. Therefore, O God, hear our prayer.*

ALL: *Bless this land of ours, O Lord. Keep watch over it and protect it from the powers of tryanny and all that oppresses the human spirit. Grant us the wisdom to use our freedom wisely, to choose our leaders well, and to work for equality and justice not only within our borders but throughout the world. In the name of Jesus we pray, amen.*

**53**

# World Day of Prayer

LEADER: Beneath the sorrow of this world, hidden in silence, coursing through channels far below this routine existence, does not a river of new wine surge and roll, longing to rise like spring sap and blossom into a song of praise, a subtle gesture of kindness, a word spoken quietly in love, a prayer said for another in secret?

PEOPLE: *O Lord, in this world we shall never know or number the countless prayers that have been offered for us by others.*

LEADER: Like an invisible tapestry they form a tabernacle stronger than the bricks of this building. In this world we spend all of our days beneath this unseen prayer shawl of unspoken prayer.

PEOPLE: *In the hearts of how many, O Lord, are we carried secretly through this world?*

LEADER: In the memories of how many is our image cherished like an infinitely rare jewel that gives out light as it is turned over and over in loving recollection?

PEOPLE: *In the hopes of how many is our pilgrimage through this world carried onward toward glory, swept forward on a laughing river toward that inland sea of peace and mirth?*

LEADER: In how many dreams of how many dreamers are we given an honored, lofty place, a place where the mutuality of gifts will be recognized, a place whose beauty and grace could only be built by the dreaming children of God?

PEOPLE: *O Lord, lead our hearts away from the burdens and turmoil and pettiness of this world into that silent expanse where we walk together with you. In the wilderness of our confusion and weakness, lead us to the places where the springs flow forth, where your spirit rises like a fountain, refreshing our souls and renewing our youth like the eagle's.*

LEADER: Then we shall know that we are your sons and your daughters, and the Scriptures will not just speak to us, but sing, and in your

55

presence we shall not just kneel, but dance.

PEOPLE

ALL: *Lord, we shall know that we belong to one another, that as captives to your love, we are bound together by cords mightier than the bonds of death, deeper than the veined ores of the earth and more permanent than the heavens themselves. Amen.*

ALL: THANKS BE TO YOU O, GOD,
FOR THE LIFE YOU GIVE,
THE REDEMPTION YOU OFFER
IN JESUS CHRIST, AND THE INVISIBLE
MOVEMENT OF YOUR SPIRIT ALL
AROUND US, CONFIRMING US IN
YOUR LOVE. AMEN.

# World Communion Sunday

LEADER: I hear the rushing of a mighty wind. Heaven draws close, and the Spirit of God pours forth upon the people.

PEOPLE: *Strengthen us, O Lord, to receive the gift promised by your Son, the gift of the Holy Spirit. As that gift has guided your people down through the ages, so let your Spirit rest upon us once again, empowering us to bring light, healing, and forgiveness to this broken world.*

LEADER: I see tongues of fire resting on God's servants, and I hear the sound of many voices raised, not in the confusion of Babel, but in the unity of God's redeeming love.

PEOPLE: *Once more, O Lord, let us speak the words of love to one another and to all creation. Let us rejoice in our individuality, but let us be unified in spirit. Once again let us speak in tongues, that all people everywhere may understand the message we bear on behalf of Jesus Christ.*

LEADER: And what, O people of God, is that message?

PEOPLE: *That God is reconciled to all humankind. That the power of love has triumphed once and for all over sin and death. That Jesus is Lord, and that he has promised forgiveness and salvation to all who seek him.*

ALL: *O Lord, you have called each one of us into your church, and we are now captives of your immeasurable love. Strengthen us as a congregation, bind us together in spirit and mutual love, and guide us by your Holy Spirit. Let each one of us be assured that here in your church, if nowhere else in this confused and contradictory world, we are loved, accepted, and redeemed. Help us to know that here in your church we are brought close to the great truth that God is love and that the power of this love will save all of us. In the name of Jesus do we pray, amen.*

# Missions Sunday

LEADER:      The heavens are telling the glory of God;
and the firmament proclaims his handiwork.
Day to day pours forth speech,
and night to night declares knowledge.[1]

PEOPLE:  *O Lord, if only we could proclaim your glory as the heavens
do! If only our testimony to your saving love could pour
forth from us like light from the sun! If only we could declare
the knowledge of your truth as boldly as do the stars!*

LEADER:  Is it not at your bidding that each of us is here this morning,
O Lord?

PEOPLE:  *Was it not for the salvation of each one of us that you dwelt
among us and suffered at our hands, even unto death?*

LEADER:  And was it not to shepherd us and guide us into eternal life that,
in the glory of resurrection, you returned to us with the words
of peace on your lips?

PEOPLE:  *Truly, our cup runneth over. Truly, here in God's house the
kingdom of God is among us and within us.*

LEADER:  But the world, O Lord, the world! Outside these walls your creation lies broken and alienated. Cruelty, bloodshed, heartbreak,
and despair stalk the children of humanity.

PEOPLE:  *Not to us alone, O Lord, were you sent. Not for us alone, O
Lord, was your body broken and your spirit quenched.
Neither for us alone did you rise in glory.*

LEADER:  The ends of the earth await the salvation of God. But whom will   **59**
God send to bear the Good News, to bind the wounds and heal
the brokenness, to speak the holy word that brings peace and
salvation to the troubled and lost?

[1]Psalm 19:1-2

PEOPLE: *Here we stand, O Lord. Open our hearts that we may receive the gift of the Holy Spirit. Whether the Spirit comes as quietly as breath exhaled or as mightily as a rushing wind, help us to receive this gift. Then, O Lord, we shall speak the miracle of your grace boldly and proclaim your glory to the ends of the world. As the sun and the stars pour light on the earth, so shall our testimony be to our brothers and sisters. Amen.*

# Litanies for Facing Challenges

We Are Not Alone
From Darkness to Light
Answering the Call of Christ
Our Gospel Journey

# We Are Not Alone

LEADER: O God, because of the faithful witness of your people down through the generations, the story of your gracious love and its sovereign power has been given to us.

We are gathered here together because we have heard the call to follow Jesus.

PEOPLE: *O Lord of grace and life and hope, help us to take the next step on our journey.*

LEADER: For when we look into ourselves and back on our past, we sometimes are overwhelmed by the failure and weakness we find, and we are gripped by fear and doubt.

PEOPLE: *But when we offer up our fearful doubt to Jesus, we are grasped and lifted up—again and again and again.*

LEADER: Yes, if we journeyed alone under our own strength, certainly the wilderness would swallow us. We would choose our way instead of being led by God to the way of life.

PEOPLE: *But we are not alone. For Jesus, the sovereign of all life, has promised that where two or more gather in his name, there he will be in their midst.*

LEADER: Where God is present with God's people, there mercy, kindness, love, and understanding flow like new wine. Lord, cast out our fears so that our hearts may be open to your love and to one another.

ALL: *In Jesus' name, amen.*

# From Darkness to Light

**LEADER:** O God, there are times when our doubts and anxieties and fears swirl around inside of us with chaotic frenzy and turmoil.

**PEOPLE:** *Sometimes the world of order and meaning that we cherish seems to be disintegrating around us, splintering and smashing apart like a fragile boat caught at sea in a mighty storm. Our world of life and light is threatened from every side, from within and from without.*

**LEADER:** Yet in the midst of our fear, in the midst of our doubt, in the midst of our faithlessness you, O Lord, are with us, calling us together to hear the gospel story, to find in each other hope and love and testimony to the gracious charity and power of God's invincible rule.

**PEOPLE:** *The light of God's gracious love, the hope that is ours in the gospel of Jesus, the faith that is our precious gift from God's merciful heart—since all of these are ours and we belong to God, let fear depart from among us and let us uncover our vulnerability and helplessness.*

**LEADER:** Yes, to fall at the feet of Jesus is not weakness or cowardice. To confess our desperation, to acknowledge our need of God's love and healing, to understand that we, in ourselves, are afraid and confused, is to show the first movements of faith.

**ALL:** *Be not afraid. Be not afraid to look into your own darkness or to dwell in the midst of the darkness around you. Neither be afraid to look into the immeasurable light of God's goodness or to pass from your darkness into that light. Be not afraid to grasp the outstretched hand and be lifted from death into life. Be not afraid to journey from sickness into health. Be not afraid to travel from fear into hope, from despair into joy.*

65

*Jesus said, "Be not afraid. Take heart. Follow me."*
*Amen.*

# Answering the Call of Christ

LEADER: We start forward, we hesitate, we turn back. We are taught but do not learn, hear, but do not understand. We speak without thinking. The bread has been broken and given to us so many times, yet still we doubt and are afraid.

PEOPLE: *You know our hearts, O God; you know our weakness and fear. But you also know the goodness in us, for we are your children. Lead us to the saving knowledge that we do not have it in us to be disciples of Jesus. Yet we confess we have heard his call.*

LEADER: The call to follow the Lord is God's invitation to enter more deeply into the mystery of grace where sorrow and joy, pain and delight, fear and beauty, meet in the healing gaze of Jesus.

PEOPLE: *Truly, we do not know ourselves well or understand either our strength or our weakness. But Jesus knows us through and through. He has chosen you and me to find our joy in following him.*

LEADER: Lord, we want to say yes to you. We want to be your disciples, but we lack courage and strength. Help us to trust our hearts knowing that you have already blessed us richly, that we might continue following you on the way.

PEOPLE: *At each moment the Lord invites us to trust more boldly in God's love, to listen with greater care and attention to God's word, to let go of our anxious need for self-protection, and to feel the strong current of the Spirit sweeping us forward into kingdom waters.*

LEADER: The tide is right, my friends; the winds of grace that have brought us together here in fellowship certainly shall bear us forward in the Lord's work. We need only weigh the anchor of fear and self-centeredness and raise the sail of faith. Look! There, shining on the sea, his garments brilliant and fluttering in the sunlight, stands the risen Christ waving us forward, saying to us, "Take courage. Don't be afraid. It is I. Follow me." Amen.

# Our Gospel Journey

LEADER:  The sunshine of Galilee seems almost like a dream of childhood. We have traveled far; we have seen much. What was once simple and carefree has become complex and burdensome. What seemed the safest route is revealed as the most perilous. What looked easy now appears impossible.

PEOPLE:  *Children, how hard it is to enter into the rule of God!*

LEADER:  My friends, we set out long ago on this pilgrimage of life. Who among us has not known the fear of the wind in angry waters? Who among us, knowing the word of obedience, has not disregarded it and gone the way of selfishness? Who among us has ears and yet has failed to hear, has eyes and yet has failed to see?

PEOPLE:  *We are not always with Jesus on our journey. We do not always choose the Lord and his way, but he is with us, even unto the end. He has chosen us.*

LEADER:  The power of God does not coerce or intimidate. It sets us free to choose between the path of life and the path of death. Therefore, let us choose to follow God, who first chose us. Or let us confess to our Lord our weakness and inadequacy to follow to the end.

PEOPLE:  *God is not the enemy of the weak. God is not the enemy of the sick. God is not the enemy of sinners.*

LEADER:  Our failure, our abandonment, our betrayal is not the end of the story. It is the beginning of our gospel journey. Whatever shadows we follow, whatever floor of smug self-confidence we go crashing through, whatever failure looms up to paralyze us in fear, the power of the gospel will rise like the sun on a spring morning and we shall find ourselves by a Galilean sea at the feet of him who chose us first.

PEOPLE:  *Let fear be cast out as darkness flees before a spring dawn. We have already passed through many storms; we have already fallen and risen many times. Out of darkness we have been led into the light of Galilee again and again.*

ALL: *Therefore, O Lord, our hearts choose you and your way again, trusting that you who called us will see us through, abide with us, and go on before us. We know that wherever we choose to go, you, O Lord, will be there before us, and the gospel word of God's unconquerable love will be the last and everlasting word we shall hear. Amen.*